Pebble® Plus

Hands-On Science Fun

How to Make a BOX GUITAR

A 4D Book

by Barbara Alpert

PEBBLE
a capstone imprint

Pebble Plus is published by Capstone Press,
1710 Roe Crest Drive, North Mankato, Minnesota 56003
www.mycapstone.com

Library of Congress Cataloging-in-Publication Data
is available on the Library of Congress website.

ISBN 978-1-9771-0225-6 (library binding)
ISBN 978-1-9771-0516-5 (paperback)
ISBN 978-1-9771-0229-4 (ebook pdf)

Editorial Credits
Carrie Braulick Sheely, editor; Sarah Bennett, designer;
Marcy Morin, scheduler and project producer;
Sarah Schuette, photo stylist and project producer;
Katy LaVigne, production specialist

Photo Credits
All photographs by Capstone Studio/Karon Dubke

Note to Parents and Teachers

The Hands-On Science Fun set supports national science
standards related to physical science. This book describes
and illustrates making a box guitar. The images support early
readers in understanding the text. The repetition of words and
phrases helps early readers learn new words. This book also
introduces early readers to subject-specific vocabulary words,
which are defined in the Glossary section. Early readers may
need assistance to read some words and to use the Table of
Contents, Glossary, Read More, Internet Sites, Critical Thinking
Questions, and Index sections of the book.

1 Ask an adult to download the app.  Capstone 4D Education

2 Scan the pages with the star.

3 Enjoy your cool stuff!

—— OR ——

Use this password at capstone4D.com

guitar02256

Printed and bound in China.
970

Table of Contents

Getting Started 4

Making a Box Guitar 6

How Does It Work? 16

Glossary 22

Read More 23

Internet Sites 23

Critical Thinking Questions 24

Index 24

Safety Note:
Please ask an adult for help
when making your box guitar.

Getting Started

Music is a group of sounds.

The sounds travel through

the air to your ear.

How do they do that?

Make a box guitar and see!

You can decorate your guitar!
Before you start, paint the cereal box and paper towel tube. Use your favorite colors. Get creative! Let them dry before starting the project.

Here's what you need:

supplies to decorate (optional):
paint, paintbrush, other craft
supplies of your choice

scissors

cereal box

paper towel tube

pencil

tape

6 rubber bands
(variety of thick and thin; the rubber bands
must be long enough to stretch around
the length of the cereal box)

straw

5

Making a Box Guitar

Cut a large hole in the front of a cereal box. It can be round or shaped like a heart.

Use the paper towel tube

to trace a circle in the middle

of the box's top. Cut it out.

Put the paper towel tube

into the hole. Tape it in place.

Now take each rubber band and gently stretch it. Stretch the rubber bands around the box. All of them should be across the hole.

Cut the straw in half. Tape one straw half on each side of the hole under the strings. The bands should be lifted. Your guitar is ready to play!

First, pluck a band. Pull it fast
and let go. Next, try strumming.
Brush your thumb over
several bands.

Now try different rubber bands.
What happens?

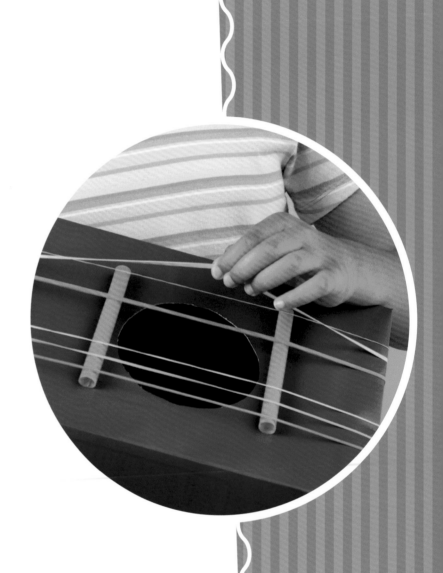

How Does It Work?

When you move a rubber band, it vibrates. Sound waves go into the hole. They bounce back out into the air. They reach your ear. You hear the sounds!

moving sound waves in air

Thin bands make short sound waves. They make a squeaky sound. They have a high pitch. Wide bands make long sound waves. They sound low, like a groan. They have a low pitch.

Tight bands also make shorter
sound waves than loose bands do.
This gives them a higher pitch.
Together, the sounds are music
to your ears!

Glossary

pitch—how high or low a sound is

pluck—to pull a guitar string quickly and let it go

strum—to brush your thumb or fingers across strings on a musical instrument

vibrate—to move back and forth quickly

sound wave—a wave or vibration that can be heard

Read More

Citro, Asia. *The Curious Kid's Science Book: 100+ Creative Hands-On Activities for Ages 4-8.* Woodinville, Wash.: Innovation Press, 2015.

Dunne, Abbie. *Sound.* Physical Science. North Mankato, Minn.: Capstone Press, 2017.

Rompella, Natalie. *Experiments in Light and Sound with Toys and Everyday Stuff.* Fun Science. North Mankato, Minn.: Capstone Press, 2017.

Internet Sites

Use FactHound to find Internet sites related to this book.

Visit *www.facthound.com*

Just type 9781977102256 and go.

Super-cool stuff!

Check out projects, games and lots more at **www.capstonekids.com**

Critical Thinking Questions

1. How is your guitar like a real guitar? How is it different?

2. Pluck a string lightly. Then pluck it hard. How does the sound change?

3. Why do you think lifting the strings helps you make music?

Index

cutting, 6, 8, 12

paper towel tubes, 8

pitch, 18, 20

plucking, 14

rubber bands, 10, 12, 14, 16, 18, 20

sound waves, 16, 18, 20

sounds, 4, 16, 18, 20

straws, 12

strumming, 14

taping, 8, 12

tracing, 8